Black & White Matrix 2

Copyright © 2010 Vincenzo Sguera

Notes | About Copyright

Published by
ARKIVIA BOOKS srl

Via Provinciale, 68
24022 Alzano Lombardo
Bergamo (Italy)
Phone: (0039) 035515851
web:
www.arkiviabooks.com
www.vincenzosguera.com
e-mail:
info@arkiviabooks.com
info@vincenzosguera.com

The DVD included is an integral part of this publication and cannot be sold separately.

CREDITS

Many thanks to these designers for their precious collaboration:
Michele Moricci, Chiara Sessa, Rosangela Fiorella,
Antonietta Casini and Nina.
They have greatly helped in developing the designs.

Vincenzo Sguera

Copyright © 2010
Vincenzo Sguera

The use of designs included in this book and in the DVD is free in accordance with the copyright terms mentioned below.
The copyright of the designs belongs to Vincenzo Sguera, who does not transfer an exclusive use. Include a line, indicating the copyright credit, everywhere possible.

The republication of this book in part or in whole and with any kind of medium (paper, CD, DVD, photocopier, Internet etc.) is forbidden except by a reviewer who may quote brief passages in a review.

The creation of designs is a continuously evolving activity. Any resemblance between the designs in this book and other designs subject to intellectual-property copyright results from ignorance of the existence of said copyright or is purely coincidental.

If, unknown to the authors and the publisher, any design contained in this book is already registered, they do not authorize the use of such design by book buyers.

They decline all responsability since they cannot be aware of all the designs registered or used previous to this publication in all countries.

All the designs in this book are ready for production and the use is free.
This is really important:
Those who buy this book can use freely the designs inside with only 3 reserves:

1)
they may not use the designs to produce a book with the same purpose and may not sell the designs in internet website.

note: they may sell their products derived from these designs but not the designs themselves.

2)
they must respect the destination of the designs.
So if a design is a texture, a different use is not authorized, such as a trademark; the same is valid for characters or graphics suitable for printing on T-shirts
These are merely ornamental designs.

3)
Each design must not already have been registered before this publication by others, as mentioned above.

Copyright belongs to
Vincenzo Sguera
who in this case cedes the use, apart from the reserves mentioned.
Thus, these designs are
not "copyright free" but "use free".

ARKIVIA BOOKS is not responsible for the use of its designs where this does not conform to the laws in force to which the user is subject.
Users assume full responsibility and should verify the real possibilities of use in their own territory of production, distribution and sales.

DVD info | Technical Details

The Book contains 1 FREE DVD with 4 FOLDERS, suitable for WINDOWS® and MACINTOSH®.

TYPE OF FILES

The Files contained in the FOLDERS 1/2 are all VECTOR :
this means in the first place that they can be opened by all softwares that use VECTOR Design. It is made up of exact lines that delimit areas where the color is uniform.
This enables the design to be brought to any size while retaining the maximum quality required.
The Files contained in the FOLDER 3 and the FOLDER 4 are all BITMAP .

SOFTWARE

The main VECTOR softwares are :
ILLUSTRATOR (the first came out in 1988), CORELDRAW and FREEHAND.
The BITMAP files (FOLDERS 3-4) can be opened in software such as PHOTOSHOP, CORELPAINT, PAINTSHOP, COREL PAINTER etc..

SIZES

The files are all real size 100%, that is, they always match the "MODULO", the part of the texture which can be repeated to infinity without discontinuity.

COLORS

In VECTOR files the single colors are flat, without transparencies or shading off.
By changing the Four Color percentages they can be modified within the software.
Each single color can be saved to prepare films, calenders, looms.

The colors used are 2: BLACK and WHITE

There are 4 FOLDERS and each one contains the same 275 textures but with different characteristics.

FOLDER 1
The Files inside are in AI Format saved for ILLUSTRATOR CS2.
There are 2 levels: in the first there is the continuous "MODULO" and in the second the "GRAPHICS" with the elements needed to edit the Pattern.

FOLDER 2
There are all the 275 MODULO TEXTURES with the same characteristics as FOLDER 1, but in AI Format saved for ILLUSTRATOR 8.
This Format it is necessary to open the files in COREL DRAW and in FREEHAND each one from version 11.

FOLDER 3
For those who want to have BITMAP Files 800 dpi, only 1 COLOR, without half-tones, PDF PHOTOSHOP Format, they are in FOLDER 3.

FOLDER 4
Here you can find Low Resolution BITMAP Files in JPG format (150 dpi in grey scale), that can be used to develop projects with lighter Files to speed up work and are for quick vision.

All files can be opened by
ILLUSTRATOR 8 and following
CORELDRAW 11 and following
FREEHAND 11 and following
PHOTOSHOP in any version.

Warning:
to avoid possible production problems with the vector files, I suggest you deactivate the overprint option, because the colors are flat and are not overprinted.

The copyright of WINDOWS, MACINTOSH, ILLUSTRATOR, CORELDRAW, FREEHAND, PHOTOSHOP, CORELPAINT, PAINTSHOP, COREL PAINTER belongs to the owners.

Black & White Matrix 2

The colours of black
are tinged with things,
objects, people, animals,
all scattered and overlapping
to generate
a modern style of textures.
A brushstroke of freshness,
no half-tones or hesitation.
Lines, silhouettes
or synthetic images
develop single themes
entering by right
into the world of decoration.

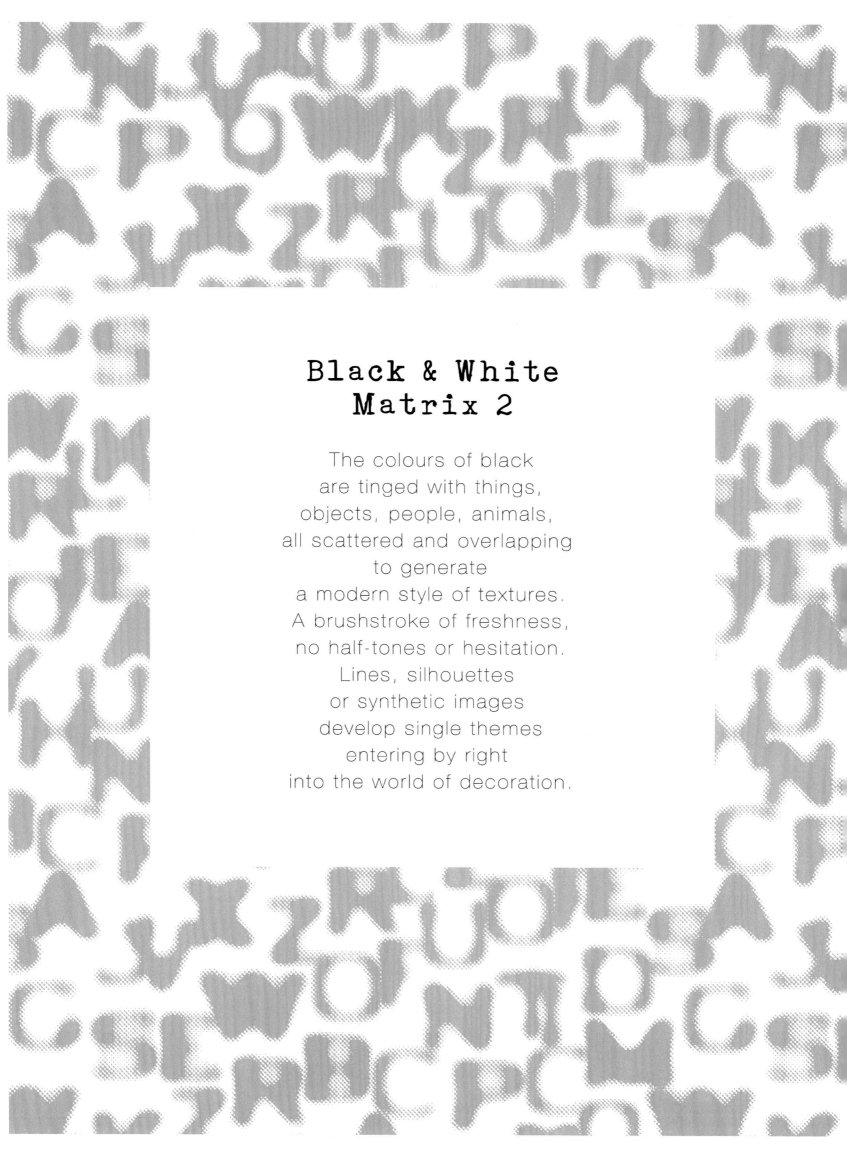

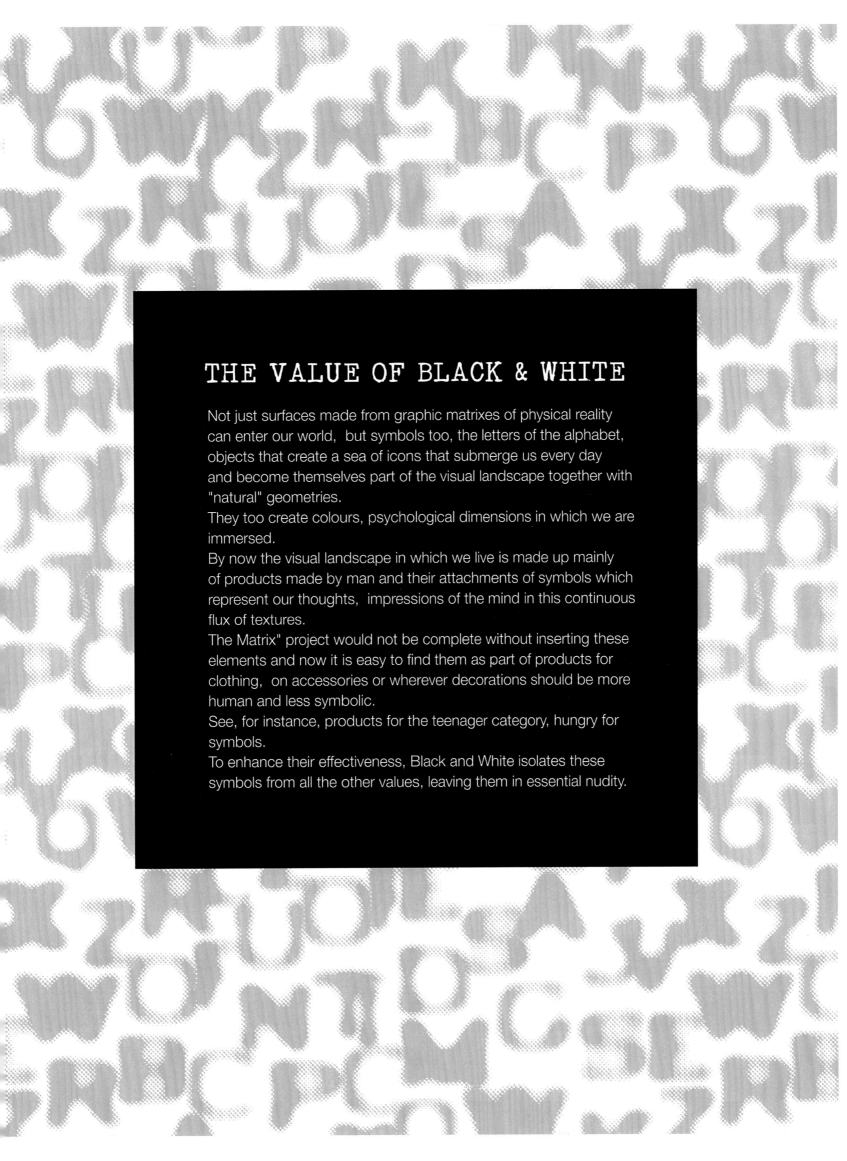

THE VALUE OF BLACK & WHITE

Not just surfaces made from graphic matrixes of physical reality can enter our world, but symbols too, the letters of the alphabet, objects that create a sea of icons that submerge us every day and become themselves part of the visual landscape together with "natural" geometries.

They too create colours, psychological dimensions in which we are immersed.

By now the visual landscape in which we live is made up mainly of products made by man and their attachments of symbols which represent our thoughts, impressions of the mind in this continuous flux of textures.

The Matrix" project would not be complete without inserting these elements and now it is easy to find them as part of products for clothing, on accessories or wherever decorations should be more human and less symbolic.

See, for instance, products for the teenager category, hungry for symbols.

To enhance their effectiveness, Black and White isolates these symbols from all the other values, leaving them in essential nudity.

BWM326 • pattern size : 200 mm x 250 mm • size on page 80%

BWM327 • pattern size : 222 mm x 222 mm • size on page 70%

pattern size : 330 mm x 216 mm • size on page 60% • BWM328

BWM329 • pattern size : 225 mm x 240 mm • size on page 80%

pattern size : 252 mm x 277 mm • size on page 100% • BWM330

BWM331 • pattern size : 310 mm x 350 mm • size on page 50%

pattern size : 245 mm x 245 mm • size on page 50% • BWM332

BWM333 • pattern size : 268 mm x 200 mm • size on page 80%

pattern size : 330 mm x 300 mm • size on page 50% • BWM334

BWM337 • pattern size : 487 mm x 276 mm • size on page 60%

pattern size : 150 mm x 150 mm • size on page 100% • BWM338

BWM339 • pattern size : 200 mm x 200 mm • size on page 100%

pattern size : 150 mm x 140 mm • size on page 100% • BWM340

BWM341 • pattern size : 335 mm x 280 mm • size on page 50%

pattern size : 380 mm x 140 mm • size on page 100% • BWM342

BWM343 • pattern size : 280 mm x 280 mm • size on page 70%

pattern size : 176 mm x 182 mm • size on page 100% • BWM344

BWM345 • pattern size : 225 mm x 200 mm • size on page 100%

pattern size : 225 mm x 200 mm • size on page 100% • BWM346

BWM347 • pattern size : 150 mm x 150 mm • size on page 60%

pattern size : 250 mm x 180 mm • size on page 100% • BWM348

BWM349 • pattern size : 235 mm x 225 mm • size on page 50%

pattern size : 280 mm x 305 mm • size on page 70% • BWM350

BWM351 • pattern size : 460 mm x 230 mm • size on page 70%

BWM353 • pattern size : 200 mm x 200 mm • size on page 100%

BWM354 • pattern size : 130 mm x 182 mm • size on page 50%

pattern size : 150 mm x 150 mm • size on page 100% • BWM355

BWM356 • pattern size : 320 mm x 350 mm • size on page 50%

pattern size : 200 mm x 200 mm • size on page 100% • BWM357

BWM358 • pattern size : 240 mm x 466 mm • size on page 70%

pattern size : 200 mm x 200 mm • size on page 60% • BWM359

page 020

BWM361 • pattern size : 400 mm x 350 mm • size on page 40%

pattern size : 300 mm x 350 mm • size on page 60% • BWM362

BWM363 • pattern size : 150 mm x 150 mm • size on page 60%

pattern size : 150 mm x 150 mm • size on page 100% • BWM364

page 022

BWM365 • pattern size : 220 mm x 210 mm • size on page 80%

BWM366 • pattern size : 200 mm x 200 mm • size on page 60%   pattern size : 315 mm x 265 mm • size on page 100% • BWM367

BWM368 • pattern size : 290 mm x 380 mm • size on page 80%

pattern size : 243 mm x 248 mm • size on page 60% • BWM369

BWM370 • pattern size : 250 mm x 250 mm • size on page 70%

pattern size : 150 mm x 150 mm • size on page 100% • BWM371

BWM372 • pattern size : 260 mm x 260 mm • size on page 100%

BWM373 • pattern size : 288 mm x 288 mm • size on page 100%

BWM374 • pattern size : 300 mm x 275 mm • size on page 60%

BWM375 • pattern size : 180 mm x 180 mm • size on page 80%

pattern size : 180 mm x 180 mm • size on page 80% • BWM376

BWM377 • pattern size : 300 mm x 300 mm • size on page 80%

pattern size : 250 mm x 280 mm • size on page 80% • BWM378

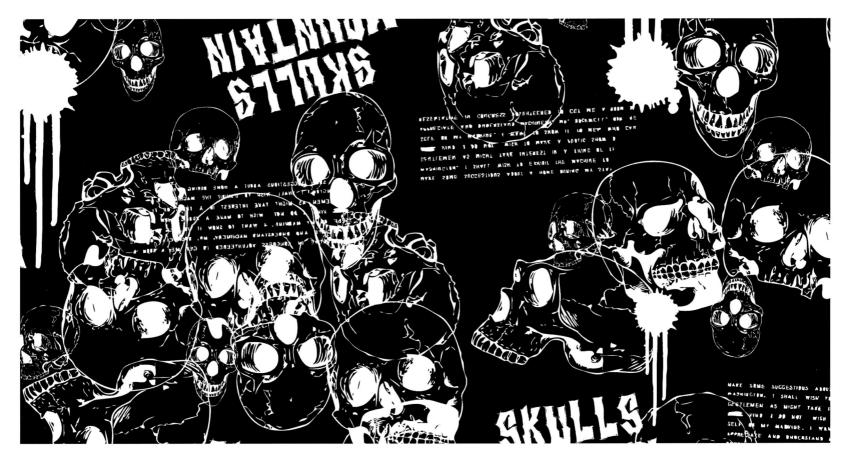

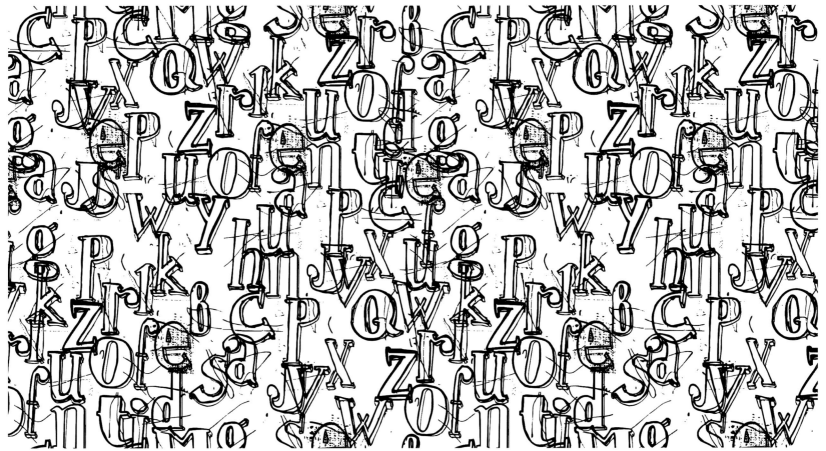

BWM379 • pattern size : 300 mm x 300 mm • size on page 60%

pattern size : 100 mm x 100 mm • size on page 120% • BWM380

BWM381 • pattern size : 150 mm x 150 mm • size on page 60%

pattern size : 300 mm x 300 mm • size on page 50% • BWM382

BWM383 • pattern size : 200mm x 200 mm • size on page 80%

pattern size : 222 mm x 230 mm • size on page 50% • BWM384

pattern size : 350 mm x 330 mm • size on page 100% • BWM385

BWM386 • pattern size : 200 mm x 200 mm • size on page 120%

BWM387 • pattern size : 100 mm x 100 mm • size on page 80%

pattern size : 150 mm x 150 mm • size on page 100% • BWM388

BWM389 • pattern size : 180 mm x 180 mm • size on page 100%

BWM390 • pattern size : 250 mm x 250 mm • size on page 50%

pattern size : 271 mm x 260 mm • size on page 50% • BWM391

BWM392 • pattern size : 180 mm x 180 mm • size on page 70%

pattern size : 180 mm x 180 mm • size on page 100% • BWM393

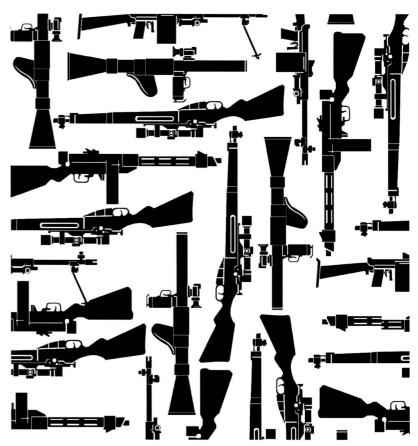

BWM395 • pattern size : 250 mm x 240 mm • size on page 70%

pattern size : 230 mm x 325 mm • size on page 50% • BWM396

BWM397 • pattern size : 180 mm x 180 mm • size on page 70%

pattern size : 258 mm x 258 mm • size on page 50% • BWM398

BWM401 • pattern size : 250 mm x 240 mm • size on page 100%

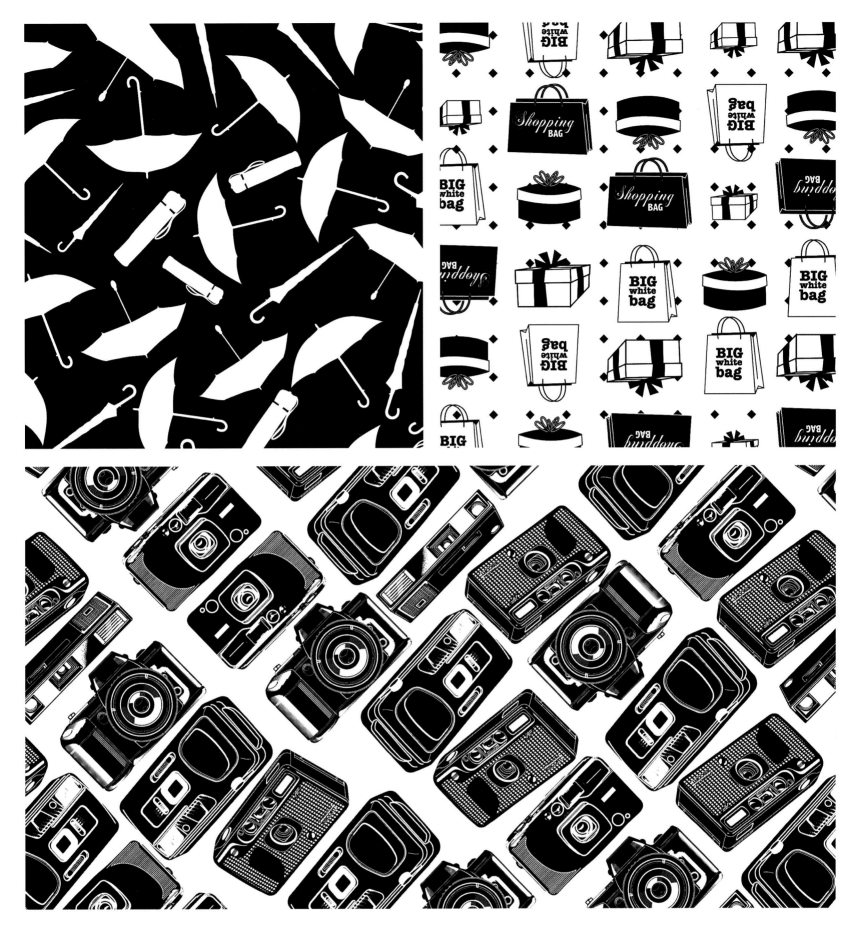

BWM402 • pattern size : 150 mm x 150 mm • size on page 85%

pattern size : 225 mm x 225 mm • size on page 70% • BWM403

BWM404 • pattern size : 220 mm x 220 mm • size on page 100%

BWM405 • pattern size : 196 mm x 216 mm • size on page 100%

pattern size : 250 mm x 250 mm • size on page 70% • BWM406

BWM407 • pattern size : 225 mm x 285 mm • size on page 100%

BWM409 • pattern size : 270 mm x 260 mm • size on page 100%

pattern size : 320 mm x 250 mm • size on page 100% • BWM410

BWM411 • pattern size : 160 mm x 190 mm • size on page 70%

pattern size : 265 mm x 270 mm • size on page 70% • BWM412

BWM413 • pattern size : 150 mm x 150 mm • size on page 100%

BWM415 • pattern size : 200 mm x 330 mm • size on page 70%

pattern size : 224 mm x 230 mm • size on page 40% • BWM416

BWM417 • pattern size : 270 mm x 245 mm • size on page 100%

BWM418 • pattern size : 230 mm x 230 mm • size on page 90%

pattern size : 260 mm x 340 mm • size on page 50% • BWM419

BWM420 • pattern size : 300 mm x 130 mm • size on page 100%

pattern size : 250 mm x 250 mm • size on page 100% • BWM421

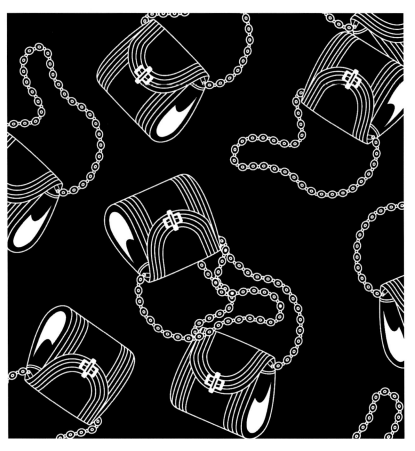

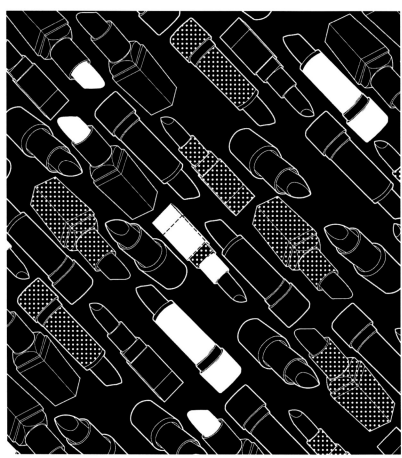

BWM422 • pattern size : 200 mm x 200 mm • size on page 70%

pattern size : 270 mm x 270 mm • size on page 50% • BWM423

BWM424 • pattern size : 250 mm x 300 mm • size on page 80%

pattern size : 400 mm x 280 mm • size on page 50% • BWM425

BWM426 • pattern size : 180 mm x 180 mm • size on page 80%

pattern size : 260 mm x 260 mm • size on page 80% • BWM427

BWM428 • pattern size : 290 mm x 220 mm • size on page 70%

BWM429 • pattern size : 260 mm x 255 mm • size on page 100%

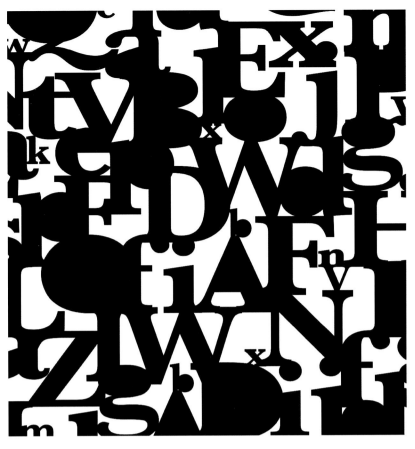

BWM430 • pattern size : 220 mm x 236 mm • size on page 100%

pattern size : 285 mm x 270 mm • size on page 60% • BWM431

BWM432 • pattern size : 180 mm x 180 mm • size on page 100%

pattern size : 200 mm x 200 mm • size on page 70% • BWM433

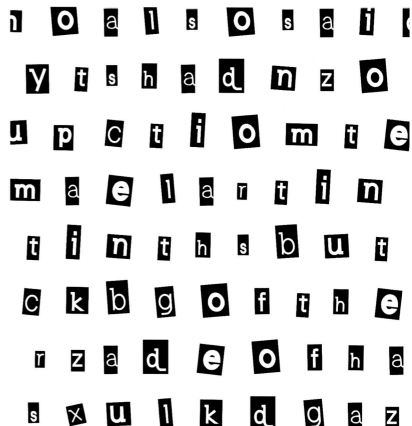
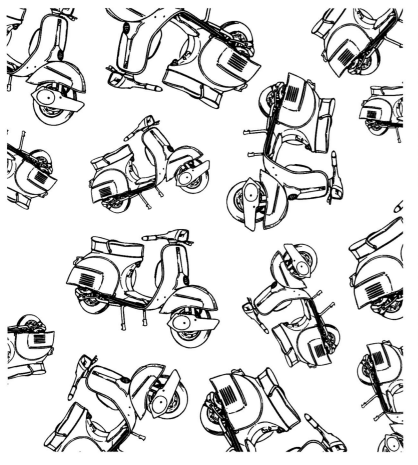

BWM434 • pattern size : 310 mm x 270 mm • size on page 70%

pattern size : 220 mm x 200 mm • size on page 70% • BWM435

BWM436 • pattern size : 150 mm x 150 mm • size on page 100%

pattern size : 180 mm x 180 mm • size on page 70% • BWM437

pattern size : 280 mm x 280 mm • size on page 100% • BWM438

BWM439 • pattern size : 210 mm x 210 mm • size on page 100%

pattern size : 175 mm x 90 mm • size on page 100% • BWM440

BWM441 • pattern size : 250 mm x 250 mm • size on page 70%

pattern size : 245 mm x 265 mm • size on page 70% • BWM442

BWM443 • pattern size : 245 mm x 230 mm • size on page 90%

pattern size : 222 mm x 222 mm • size on page 85% • BWM444

BWM445 • pattern size : 250 mm x 280 mm • size on page 100%

BWM446 • pattern size : 270 mm x 260 mm • size on page 80%

BWM447 • pattern size : 350 mm x 290 mm • size on page 60%

pattern size : 200 mm x 200 mm • size on page 80% • BWM448

BWM449 • pattern size : 270 mm x 290 mm • size on page 50%

pattern size : 250 mm x 335 mm • size on page 50% • BWM450

BWM451 • pattern size : 288 mm x 340 mm • size on page 50%

pattern size : 200 mm x 200 mm • size on page 80% • BWM452

BWM454 • pattern size : 350 mm x 315 mm • size on page 80%

BWM455 • pattern size : 120 mm x 100 mm • size on page 80%

pattern size : 150 mm x 150 mm • size on page 80% • BWM456

BWM457 • pattern size : 230 mm x 215 mm • size on page 100%

BWM458 • pattern size : 212 mm x 232 mm • size on page 50%

pattern size : 200 mm x 200 mm • size on page 80% • BWM459

BWM460 • pattern size : 230 mm x 235 mm • size on page 80%

pattern size : 238 mm x 266 mm • size on page 50% • BWM461

BWM464 • pattern size : 240 mm x 280 mm • size on page 70%

pattern size : 205 mm x 255 mm • size on page 60% • BWM465

BWM466 • pattern size : 262 mm x 269 mm • size on page 80%

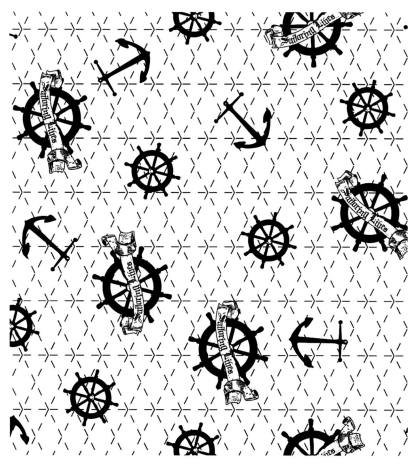

BWM467 • pattern size : 150 mm x 150 mm • size on page 80%

pattern size : 200 mm x 230 mm • size on page 70% • BWM468

BWM469 • pattern size : 280 mm x 300 mm • size on page 50%

pattern size : 240 mm x 240 mm • size on page 50% • BWM470

BWM473 • pattern size : 220 mm x 245 mm • size on page 70%

pattern size : 200 mm x 180 mm • size on page 60% • BWM474

BWM475 • pattern size : 225 mm x 225 mm • size on page 70%

pattern size : 450 mm x 350 mm • size on page 40% • BWM476

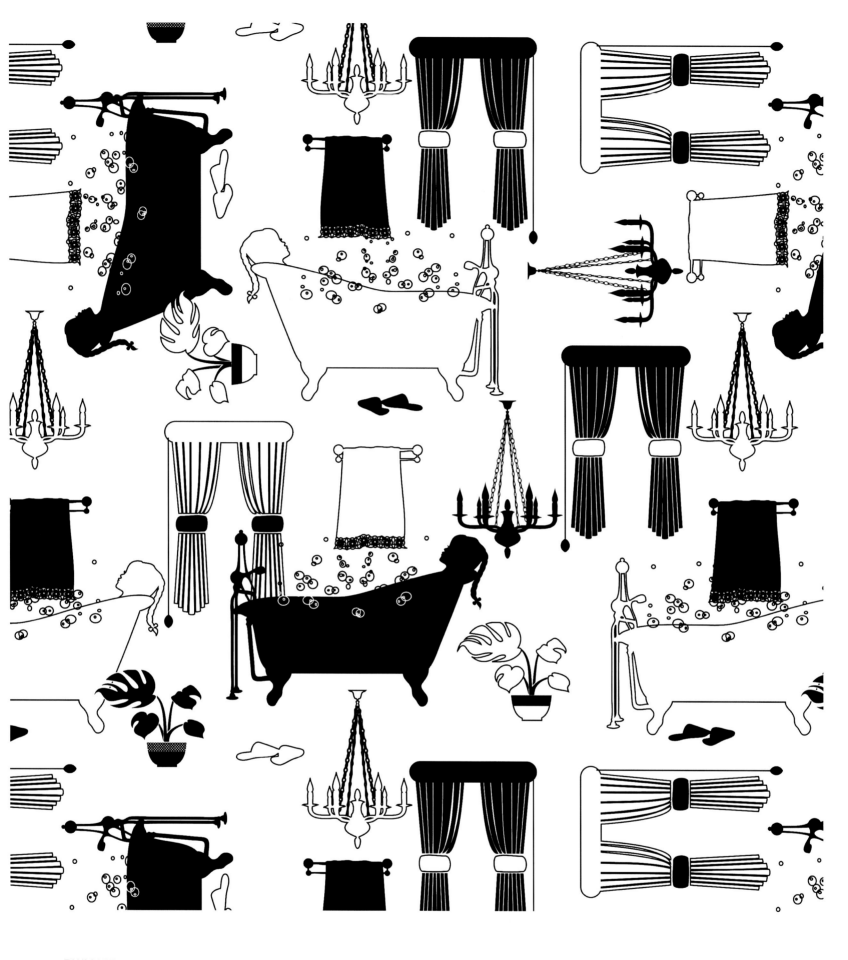

BWM477 • pattern size : 250 mm x 250 mm • size on page 80%

BWM478 • pattern size : 200 mm x 200 mm • size on page 60%

pattern size : 200 mm x 200 mm • size on page 60% • BWM479

BWM480 • pattern size : 200 mm x 200 mm • size on page 60%

BWM481 • pattern size : 350 mm x 350 mm • size on page 70%

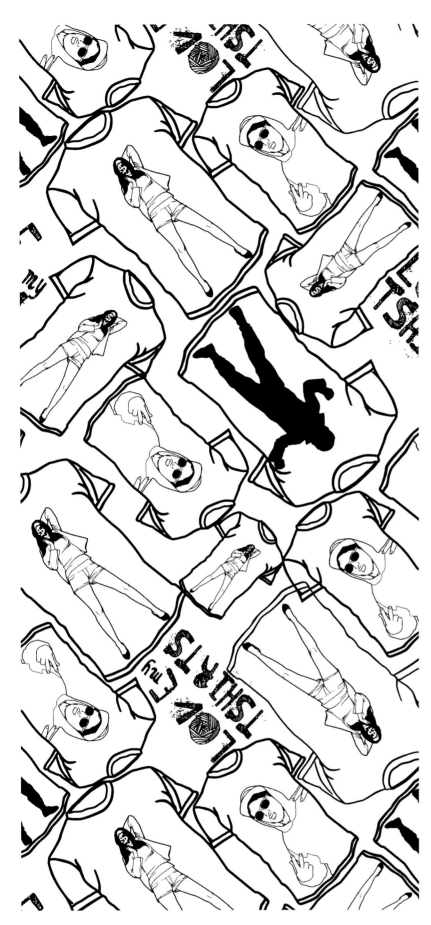

BWM482 • pattern size : 265 mm x 265 mm • size on page 70%

pattern size : 220 mm x 220 mm • size on page 70% • BWM483

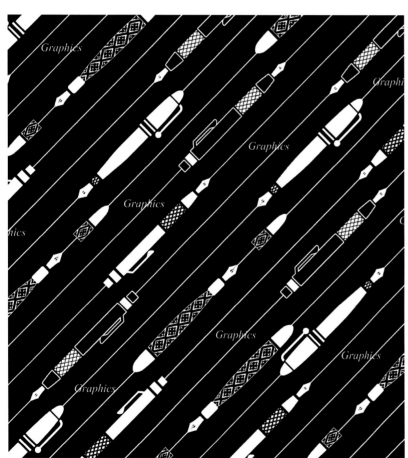

BWM484 • pattern size : 180 mm x 200 mm • size on page 50%

pattern size : 180 mm x 180 mm • size on page 70% • BWM485

BWM486 • pattern size : 200 mm x 200 mm • size on page 60%

pattern size : 200 mm x 200 mm • size on page 60% • BWM487

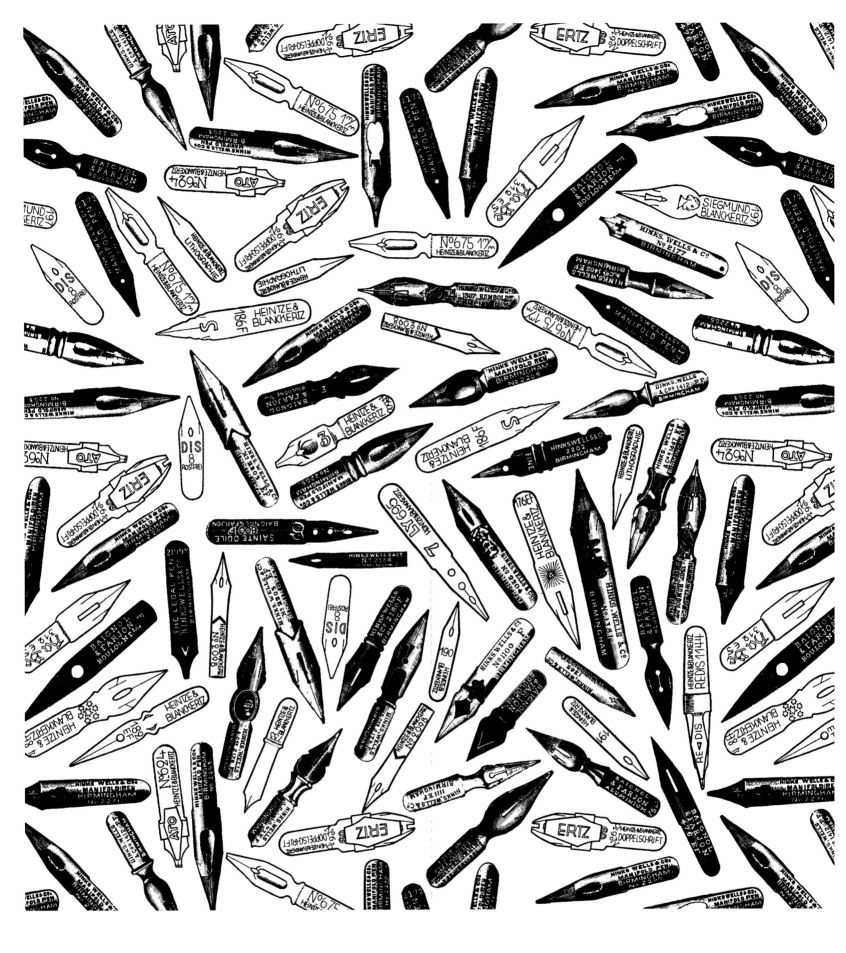

BWM490 • pattern size : 230 mm x 230 mm • size on page 60%

pattern size : 150 mm x 150 mm • size on page 70% • BWM491

BWM492 • pattern size : 180 mm x 180 mm • size on page 80%

pattern size : 180 mm x 180 mm • size on page 60% • BWM493

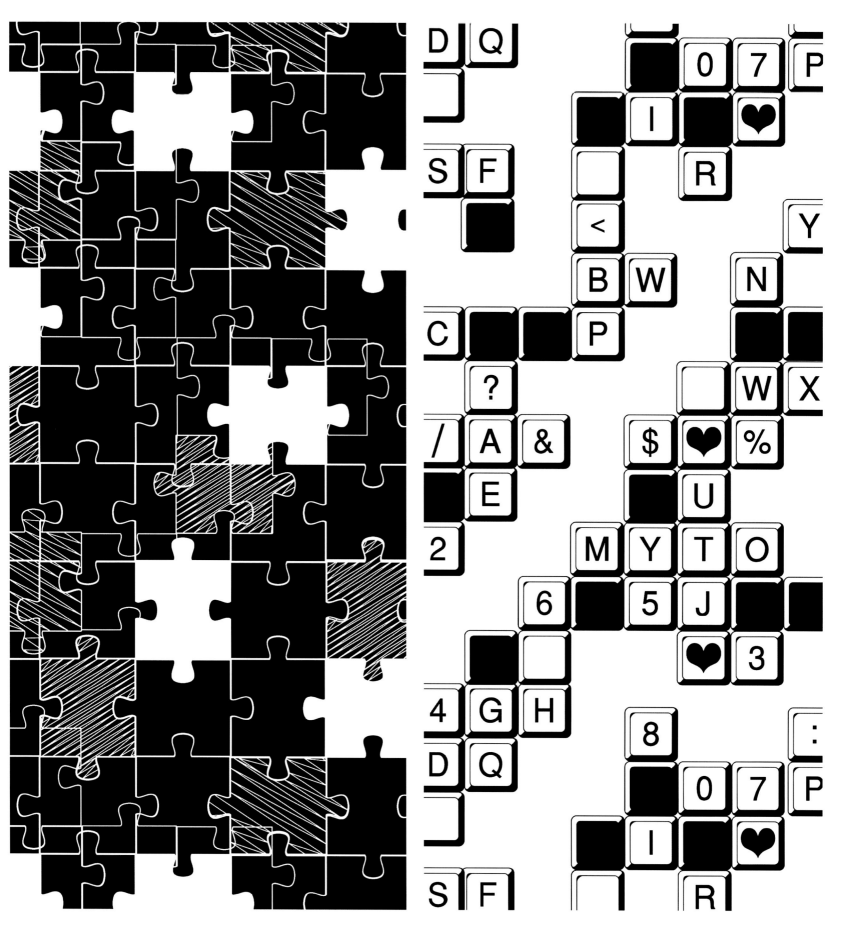

BWM496 • pattern size : 480 mm x 480 mm • size on page 40%

pattern size : 300 mm x 300 mm • size on page 60% • BWM497

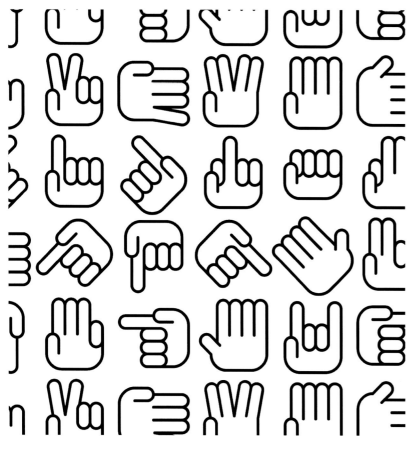

BWM498 • pattern size : 270 mm x 180 mm • size on page 50%

pattern size : 166 mm x 114 mm • size on page 80% • BWM499

BWM500 • pattern size : 180 mm x 180 mm • size on page 60%

pattern size : 240 mm x 240 mm • size on page 60% • BWM501

BWM503 • pattern size : 225 mm x 250 mm • size on page 100%

BWM504 • pattern size : 300 mm x 285 mm • size on page 60%

BWM505 • pattern size : 200 mm x 220 mm • size on page 60%

pattern size : 300 mm x 300 mm • size on page 60% • BWM506

BWM507 • pattern size : 400 mm x 290 mm • size on page 70%   pattern size : 280 mm x 280 mm • size on page 60% • BWM508

BWM509 • pattern size : 200 mm x 200 mm • size on page 60%   pattern size : 300 mm x 300 mm • size on page 70% • BWM510

BWM513 • pattern size : 235 mm x 250 mm • size on page 100%

pattern size : 300 mm x 240 mm • size on page 80% • BWM514

BWM515 • pattern size : 250 mm x 250 mm • size on page 70%

pattern size : 300 mm x 400 mm • size on page 70% • BWM516

BWM517 • pattern size : 150 mm x 150 mm • size on page 80%   pattern size : 285 mm x 285 mm • size on page 80% • BWM518

BWM519 • pattern size : 250 mm x 250 mm • size on page 100%

pattern size : 200 mm x 200 mm • size on page 100% • BWM520

BWM521 • pattern size : 400 mm x 200 mm • size on page 100%

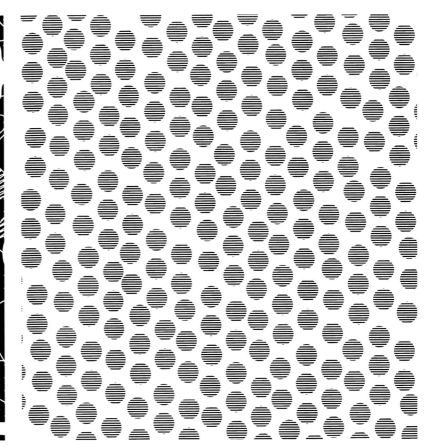
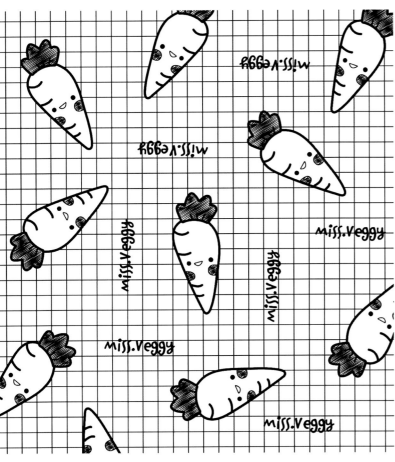

BWM522 • pattern size : 325 mm x 225 mm • size on page 70%

pattern size : 250 mm x 350 mm • size on page 70% • BWM523

BWM524 • pattern size : 250 mm x 260 mm • size on page 60%

pattern size : 200 mm x 260 mm • size on page 60% • BWM525

091 page

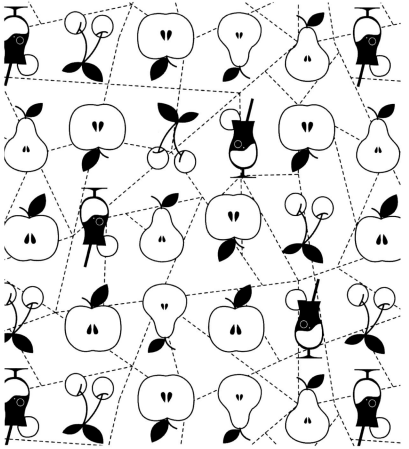

BWM526 • pattern size : 240 mm x 250 mm • size on page 70%

BWM527 • pattern size : 200 mm x 200 mm • size on page 50%

pattern size : 200 mm x 200 mm • size on page 70% • BWM528

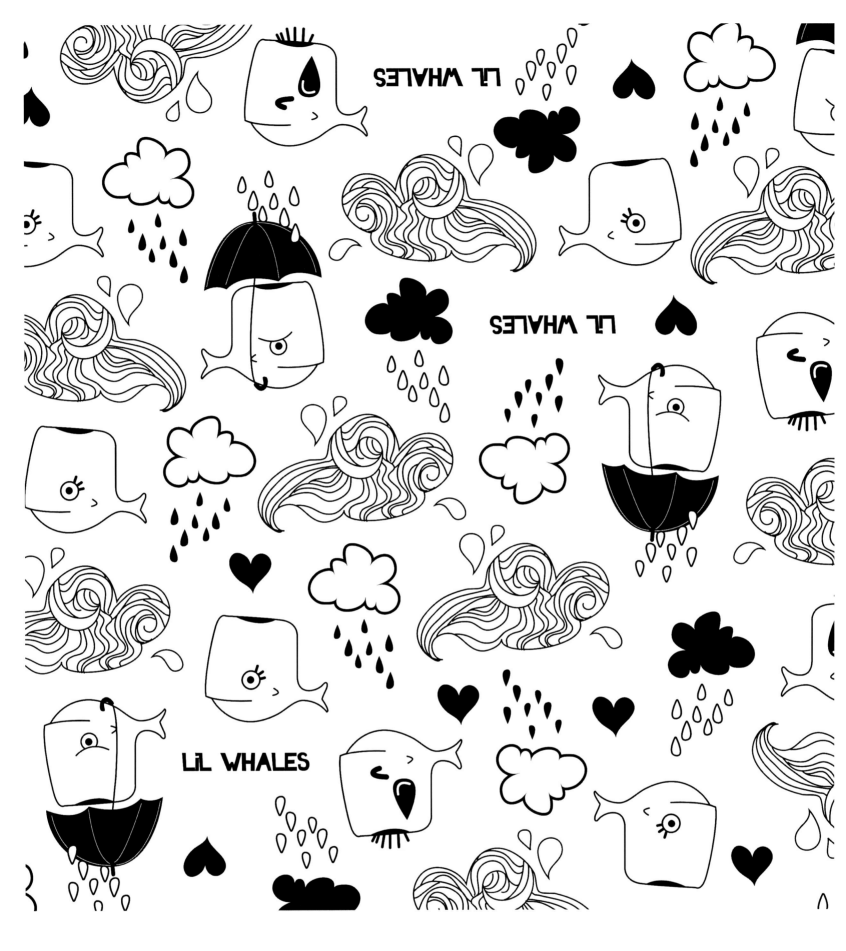

BWM530 • pattern size : 260 mm x 260 mm • size on page 100%

BWM531 • pattern size : 240 mm x 270 mm • size on page 60%

pattern size : 270 mm x 220 mm • size on page 80% • BWM532

BWM533 • pattern size : 180 mm x 180 mm • size on page 80%

BWM535 • pattern size : 60 mm x 60 mm • size on page 200%

pattern size : 260 mm x 250 mm • size on page 60% • BWM536

BWM537 • pattern size : 250 mm x 250 mm • size on page 80%

BWM538 • pattern size : 325 mm x 285 mm • size on page 80%

pattern size : 240 mm x 220 mm • size on page 100% • BWM539

BWM540 • pattern size : 135 mm x 135 mm • size on page 100%

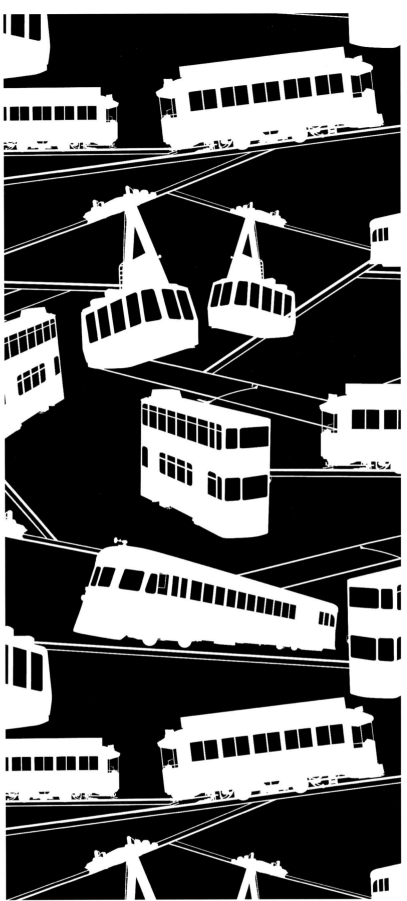

pattern size : 180 mm x 180 mm • size on page 100% • BWM541

BWM542 • pattern size : 150 mm x 150 mm • size on page 100%

pattern size : 180 mm x 180 mm • size on page 100% • BWM543

BWM544 • pattern size : 140 mm x 140 mm • size on page 100%

pattern size : 120 mm x 234 mm • size on page 100% • BWM545

pattern size : 250 mm x 300 mm • size on page 100% • BWM546

BWM552 • pattern size : 250 mm x 250 mm • size on page 60%

pattern size : 180 mm x 180 mm • size on page 70% • BWM553

BWM554 • pattern size : 200 mm x 200 mm • size on page 60%

pattern size : 200 mm x 200 mm • size on page 60% • BWM555

BWM556 • pattern size : 230 mm x 230 mm • size on page 100%

BWM557 • pattern size : 200 mm x 200 mm • size on page 60%

pattern size : 250 mm x 250 mm • size on page 60% • BWM558

BWM559 • pattern size : 290 mm x 270 mm • size on page 60%

pattern size : 180 mm x 180 mm • size on page 60% • BWM560

BWM561 • pattern size : 225 mm x 225 mm • size on page 80%

BWM562 • pattern size : 230 mm x 250 mm • size on page 60%

pattern size : 270 mm x 240 mm • size on page 80% • BWM563

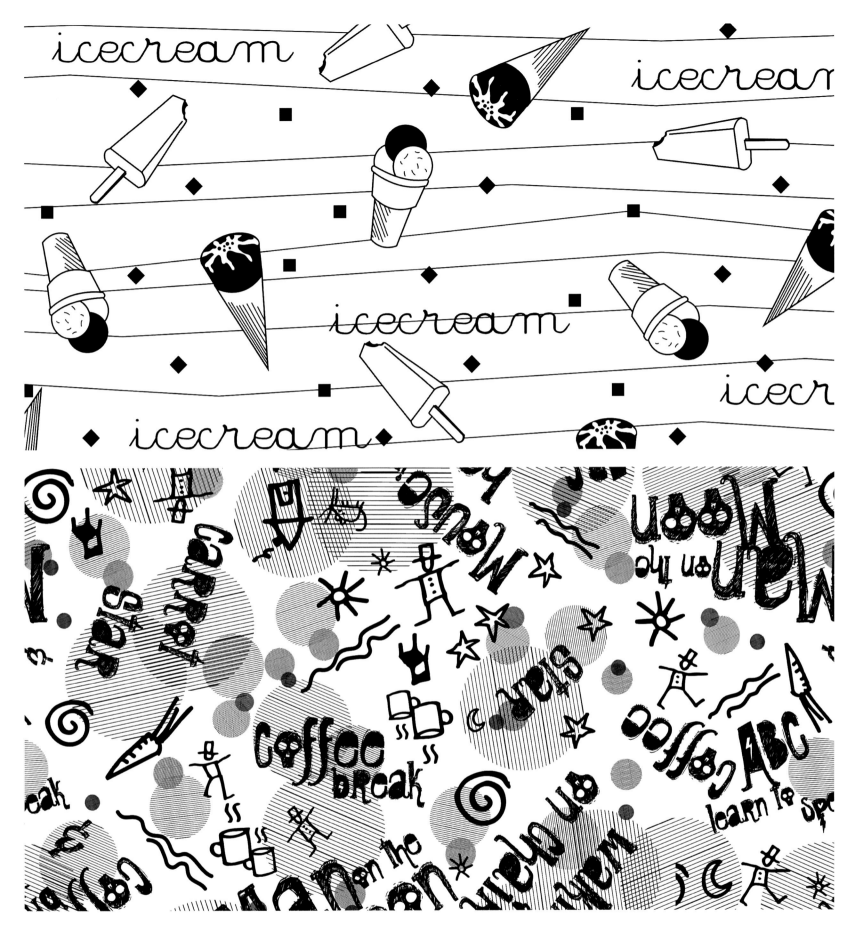

BWM564 • pattern size : 476 mm x 244 mm • size on page 70%

pattern size : 325 mm x 250 mm • size on page 70% • BWM565

BWM566 • pattern size : 300 mm x 300 mm • size on page 60%

BWM567 • pattern size : 270 mm x 275 mm • size on page 60%

pattern size : 243 mm x 250 mm • size on page 60% • BWM568

pattern size : 245 mm x 245 mm • size on page 80% • BWM569

BWM570 • pattern size : 250 mm x 250 mm • size on page 100%

BWM571 • pattern size : 100 mm x 84 mm • size on page 100%

pattern size : 330 mm x 330 mm • size on page 50% • BWM572

pattern size : 290 mm x 270 mm • size on page 100% • BWM573

BWM574 • pattern size : 250 mm x 280 mm • size on page 80%

BWM575 • pattern size : 180 mm x 180 mm • size on page 80%

pattern size : 150 mm x 150 mm • size on page 80% • BWM576

pattern size : 260 mm x 260 mm • size on page 90% • BWM577

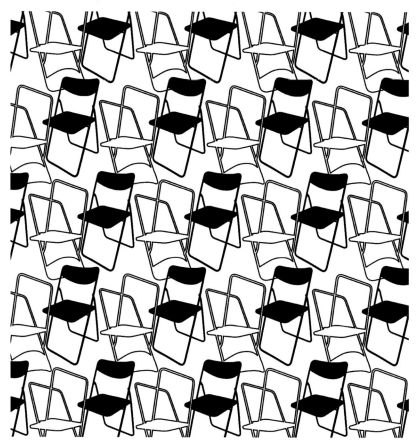
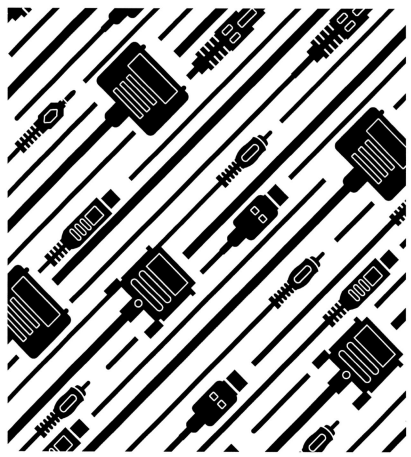

BWM578 • pattern size : 174 mm x 116 mm • size on page 80%

pattern size : 180 mm x 156 mm • size on page 40% • BWM579

BWM580 • pattern size : 200 mm x 160 mm • size on page 100%

pattern size : 200 mm x 200 mm • size on page 80% • BWM581

pattern size : 336 mm x 264 mm • size on page 100% • BWM582

BWM584 • pattern size : 270 mm x 315 mm • size on page 60%

pattern size : 200 mm x 200 mm • size on page 60% • BWM585

BWM586 • pattern size : 200 mm x 200 mm • size on page 60%

pattern size : 350 mm x 365 mm • size on page 60% • BWM587

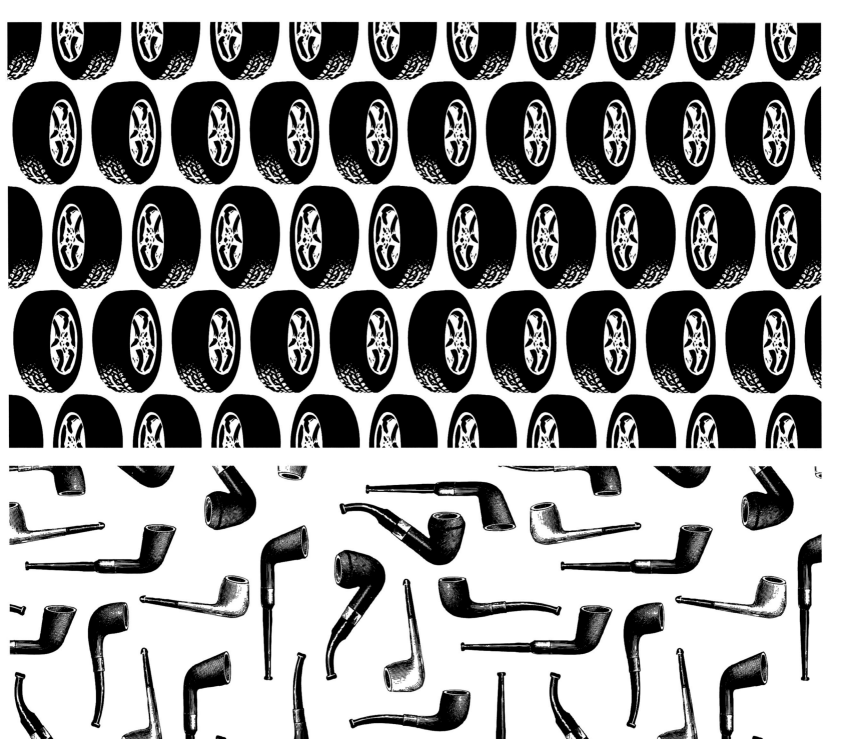

BWM588 • pattern size : 196 mm x 216 mm • size on page 80%

pattern size : 190 mm x 190 mm • size on page 80% • BWM589

pattern size : 190 mm x 190 mm • size on page 100% • BWM590

BWM591 • pattern size : 200 mm x 200 mm • size on page 70%

BWM592 • pattern size : 116 mm x 116 mm • size on page 100%

pattern size : 170 mm x 185 mm • size on page 70% • BWM593

BWM594 • pattern size : 100 mm x 100 mm • size on page 100%

pattern size : 350 mm x 350 mm • size on page 70% • BWM595

BWM597 • pattern size : 100 mm x 100 mm • size on page 100%

pattern size : 150 mm x 150 mm • size on page 100% • BWM598

BWM599 • pattern size : 250 mm x 250 mm • size on page 60%

pattern size : 400 mm x 260 mm • size on page 60% • BWM600

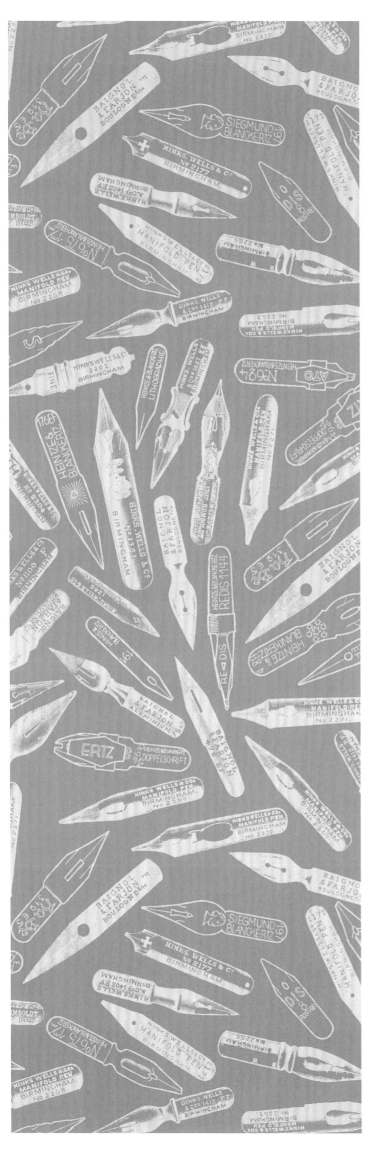

Arkivia Books
collection

WHY ARKIVIA BOOKS?

For those who work as stylists or designers of product lines in various merceological sectors, one of the most important jobs is to determine the look that the line should have to attract clients and distinguish itself from others.

Research is fundamental, before any design can be made, research using books, magazines, samples of objects found all over the world. This results in a large quantity of ideas on which the marketing department works before starting to develop one of them.
A long and expensive process to reach the development of the designs, keeping in mind the production methods.

I have inserted into my books this kind of know-how:

1 - Research into a tendency theme
2 - Development of creative ideas that illustrate it
3 - Professional artworks for immediate production with that look.

WHO FINDS ARKIVIA BOOKS USEFUL?

1 - Those who create products every day and need to document a single theme suitable to the product.
2 - Companies that with a small amount of money, very low compared with the high costs of creative studios, can access material ready to be used and developed by their internal staff.

In the recent past, Tendency Books have been produced for a restricted club of professional people who could afford the high cost of this sort of book
(around 1000/1500 euros).
I have decided to create books with the same spirit but within the reach of any professional in image.
As expensive as a good quality book but no more than is accepted in bookshops.

SOME TECHNICAL INFORMATION

All files in the CD or in DVD are in hi-res format:
PHOTOSHOP PDF format for bitmap files or
ILLUSTRATOR format for vector files, accessible by all programmes and compatible with WINDOWS and MAC.

All vectorial files are modifiable because they are the original graphics and the material is produced in a professional way and ready to use.

The designs are free to be used by those who buy the books in accordance with copyright terms present in each book.

Vincenzo Sguera

Tecno Pop Graphics vol.1

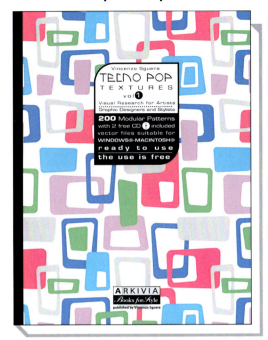

ISBN 9788888766010
HARDBACK • 144 pages
size 24cm x 30.7cm
200 TEXTURES saved
in 4 ways 800 files in all

2 Free CDs included
for WINDOWS and MAC
Vector and Bitmap Files
Ready for Production.
The use is Free

200 textures in the new POP style, using simple and geometric shapes.
This collection is intended for textile fabrics in clothing and home furniture. But also some designs are suitable for wrapping and wallpaper or for stationery, packaging and accessory collections.

Optical Textures vol.1

ISBN 9788888766027
PAPERBACK • 128 pages
size 24cm x 30.7cm
112 TEXTURES saved
in 4 ways-448 files in all

1 Free CD included
for WINDOWS and MAC
Vector and Bitmap Files
Ready for Production.
The use is Free

This book develops ideas inspired by "OP ART"
The most part of these textures is based on tricks of visual perception: using rules of perspective to give the illusion of three-dimensional space.
Op art works are usually abstract, with many of the better known pieces made in only black and white.

Styling Book vol.1

ISBN 9788888766034 HARDBACK Edition
ISBN 9788888766515 PAPERBACK Edition
144 pages) • size 24cm x 30.7cm
229 MODEL SHEETS • plus PRINTS, TEXTURES
2 CDs or 1 DVD included for WINDOWS and MAC.
Vector Files • The use is Free.

The 16 families of characters have been developed all in a fresh and modern style. Real model sheets can be used for graphic needs.

You can move parts of them to create other positions since they are created in Adobe Illustrator with separable parts (body, arms, head, eyes etc).

Junior Pop Textures vol.1

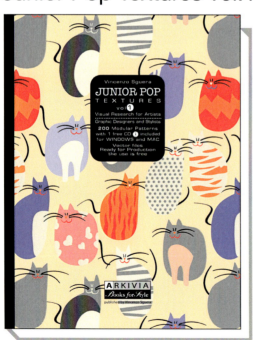

ISBN 9788888766041 HARDBACK Edition
ISBN 9788888766522 PAPERBACK Edition
144 pages • size 24cm x 30.7cm
200 TEXTURES saved in 2 ways-400 files in all.
1 Free CD included for WINDOWS and MAC.
Vector Files • The use is Free.

This book develops textures in the new POP Style. Textures for kids and teenagers, using characters and shapes, simple and geometric.

Designs useful for textile fabrics, for clothing and home furniture, wall and gift papers, gadgets and stationery items.

Styling Book vol.2

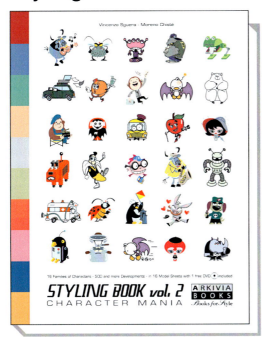
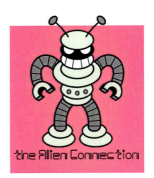

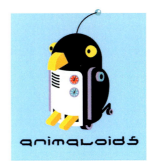

ISBN 9788888766058 HARDBACK Edition
ISBN 9788888766539 PAPERBACK Edition
160 pages • size 24cm x 30.7cm
More than 500 designs with 1 DVD included
Vector Files • The use is Free.

The 16 families of characters have been developed all in a fresh and modern style. Real model sheets can be used for graphic needs.

You can move parts of them to create other positions since they are created in Adobe Illustrator with separable parts (body, arms, head, eyes etc).

New Age Textures vol.1

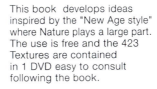

ISBN 9788888766003 HARDBACK Edition
ISBN 9788888766065 PAPERBACK Edition
144 pages) • size 24cm x 30.7cm
423 TEXTURES saved for WINDOWS and MAC
3 CDs or 1 DVD with EPS Bitmap Files (300 dpi).
CMYK-300 dpi resolution • The use is Free.

This book develops ideas inspired by the "New Age style" where Nature plays a large part. The use is free and the 423 Textures are contained in 1 DVD easy to consult following the book.

It reproduces all the designs in natural format, indicates the full development of the module and the textures are already set to be repeated to infinity in perfect alignment.

Gothic Pop Textures vol.1

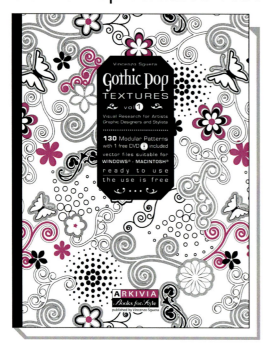

ISBN 9788888766072 HARDBACK Edition
ISBN 9788888766546 PAPERBACK Edition
144 pages • size 24cm x 30.7cm
130 TEXTURES saved in 4 ways-520 files in all.
I Free DVD included for WINDOWS and MAC.
Vector and Bitmap Files • The use is Free.

This book develops textures in the new GOTHIC taste. From the Neo Floreal and Liberty Style, soft-coloured or black and white textures.

Designs useful for textile fabrics, for clothing and home furniture, wall and gift papers, gadgets and stationery items.

Gothic Pop Textures vol.2

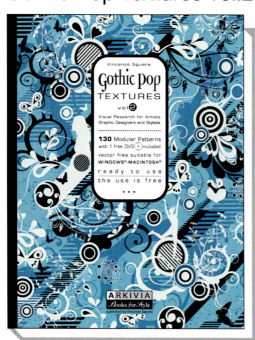

ISBN 9788888766089
HARDBACK • 144 pages
size 24cm x 30.7cm
130 TEXTURES saved
in 5 ways-650 files in all

1 Free DVD included
for WINDOWS and MAC
Vector and Bitmap Files
Ready for Production.
The use is Free

This second volume develops further designs in neo-gothic style. It too is inspired by modern and floral liberty,

but with the accent on pop: less elegant, but fresh and younger. More contaminations of various styles, colors and more creative freedom.

Character Styling vol.1 - the Cat

ISBN 9788888766096
HARDBACK • 72 pages
size 24cm x 30.7cm
149 MODEL SHEETS
54 PRINTS
14 TEXTURES

1 Free CD included for WINDOWS and MAC Vector and Bitmap Files Ready for Production. The use is Free

This BOOK, the first of a new series has an ambitious objective: to develop new characters and to teach how to create them.

Each title will develop one theme at a time but with different ways of characterizing them. I will show how to construct the basic forms.

Gothic Pop Graphics vol.1

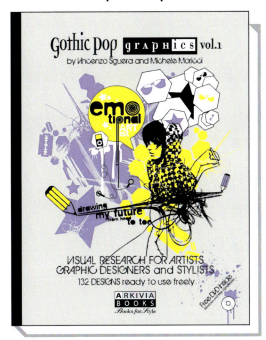

ISBN 9788888766102
HARDBACK • 144 pages
size 24cm x 30.7cm
132 GRAPHICS in 3 color variations saved in 5 ways
1980 files in all

1 Free DVD included for WINDOWS and MAC Vector and Bitmap Files Ready for Production. The use is Free

Prints and Logos for all sorts of use, in the style that characterizes the "ten years style" of the century.

A flow of creativity in counterpoint to the past from which it freely culls elements in a fluid and artistic way.

Natural Pop Textures vol.1

ISBN 9788888766119 HARDBACK Edition
ISBN 9788888766553 PAPERBACK Edition
144 pages • size 24cm x 30.7cm
130 TEXTURES saved in 5 ways - 650 files in all.
I Free DVD included for WINDOWS and MAC.
Vector and BitmapFiles • The use is Free.

130 elegant textures, composed with a light touch and grace. A breath of natural modernity, with their concise and linear signs.

Delicate, tonal colours that can be used from clothing to interior decorating, from accessories to wallpapering.

Natural Pop Graphics vol.1

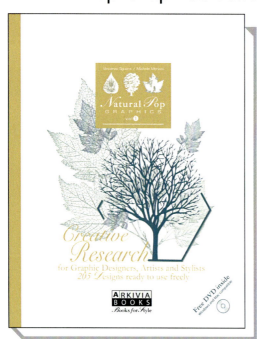

ISBN 9788888766126 HARDBACK Edition
ISBN 9788888766560 PAPERBACK Edition
144 pages • size 24cm x 30.7cm
205 GRAPHICS saved in 5 ways - 1025 files in all.
I Free DVD included for WINDOWS and MAC.
Vector and BitmapFiles • The use is Free.

Prints and Logos for all sorts of use, with a light touch and grace. A breath of natural modernity.

All the designs are vectorial. They can be used with many graphic softwares, such as ILLUSTRATOR.

Character Styling vol.2-the Bear

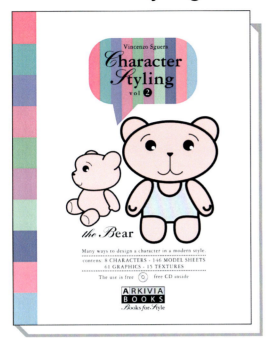

ISBN 9788888766133
HARDBACK • 72 pages
size 24cm x 30.7cm
146 MODEL SHEETS
61 PRINTS
15 TEXTURES

1 Free CD included
for WINDOWS and MAC
Vector and Bitmap Files
Ready for Production.
The use is Free

This BOOK is the 2nd of this series and I have increased the numbers of Characters to 8. I wanted to develop more Character ideas to offer a wider choice of use and style. For each one I will show how to construct the basic forms, the psychological and chromatic characteristics.

Black & White Matrix 1

ISBN 9788888766140 HARDBACK Edition
ISBN 9788888766577 PAPERBACK Edition
144 pages • size 24cm x 30.7cm
325 TEXTURES saved in 5 ways - 1625 files in all.
I Free DVD included for WINDOWS and MAC.
Vector and BitmapFiles • The use is Free.

A symphony of BLACK and WHITE, unending geometries in a mosiac full of structures as fabrics are, to satisfy our need for B&W. 325 vectorial designs where the development of one generates others in an explosion of ideas ready and available for free use.

Matrix Graphix 1

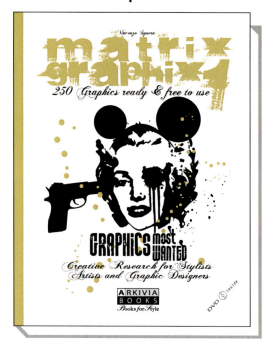

ISBN 9788888766157
HARDBACK • 144 pages
size 24cm x 30.7cm
250 GRAPHICS saved
in 5 ways 1250 files in all.

1 Free DVD included
for WINDOWS and MAC
Vector and Bitmap Files
Ready for Production.
The use is Free

The spirit of the time and the memory of the fizzy 80's have produced a miracle of sorts: a synthetical look with one color for each graphic.

More life and passion, a flow of strong flavours, with ideas that speak of yesterday but of tomorrow, too.

Black & White Matrix 2

ISBN 9788888766164 HARDBACK Edition
ISBN 9788888766584 PAPERBACK Edition
144 pages • size 24cm x 30.7cm
275 TEXTURES saved in 5 ways - 1375 files in all.
I Free DVD included for WINDOWS and MAC.
Vector and BitmapFiles • The use is Free.

This time, the colours of black are tinged with things, objects, people, animals, all scattered and overlapping to generate a modern style of textures

A brushstroke of freshness, no half-tones, lines, silhouettes or synthetic images develop single themes, entering by right into the world of decoration.

Teen Girl Graphics Vol.1

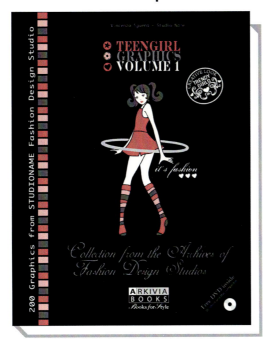

ISBN 9788888766171 HARDBACK Edition
ISBN 9788888766591 PAPERBACK Edition
96 pages • size 24cm x 30.7cm
200 GRAPHICS saved in 5 ways - 1000 files in all.
I Free DVD included for WINDOWS and MAC.
Vector and BitmapFiles.

This book is the first of a series dedicated to Stylistic Studios which have produced so much creativity, applied to the market and used by countless firms. This project stems from a studio with many years of experience which has agreed to make public its fantastic work.

Ultra Pop Textures vol.1

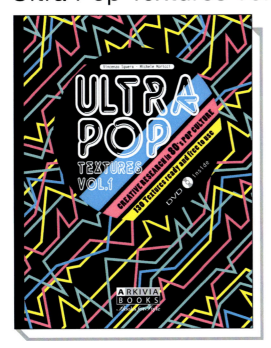

ISBN 9788888766188
HARDBACK • 144 pages
size 24cm x 30.7cm
250 TEXTURES saved
in 5 ways-1250 files in all

1 Free DVD included
for WINDOWS and MAC
Vector and Bitmap Files
Ready for Production.
The use is Free

The essence of the eighties, strong and varied, is the mix. Even in a provocative way in order to find new roads, roads that have signposted the present time, such as the Postmodern Look in contraposition to the elegant Minimalism of HI-TECH or Optical matched with Floreal, geometries and chaotic puzzles.

Ultra Pop Graphics vol.1

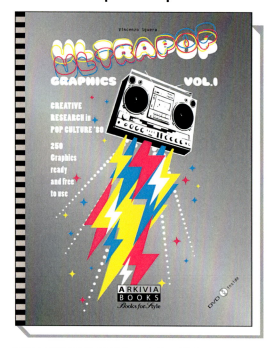

ISBN 9788888766195
HARDBACK • 144 pages
size 24cm x 30.7cm
250 GRAPHICS saved in
5 ways - 1250 files in all.

1 Free DVD included
for WINDOWS and MAC
Vector and Bitmap Files
Ready for Production.
The use is Free

The essence of the eighties, strong and varied, is the mix. Even in a provocative way in order to find new roads, roads that have signposted the present time, such as the Postmodern Look in contraposition to the elegant Minimalism of HI-TECH or Optical matched with Floreal, geometries and chaotic puzzles.

Junior Pop Graphics Vol.1

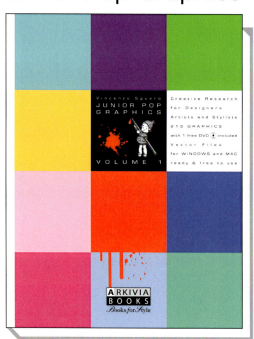

ISBN 9788888766201
HARDBACK • 96 pages
size 24cm x 30.7cm
213 TEXTURES saved
in 5 ways-1065 files in all

1 Free DVD included
for WINDOWS and MAC
Vector and Bitmap Files
Ready for Production.
The use is Free

Graphics for children that portray our world in a happy way, without dramatization and full of joy and delight.

On every page a Unique Brand, a strong idea to depart from and as we know, for a creative person, the world of children is a journey without end.

Ethno Pop Textures Vol.1

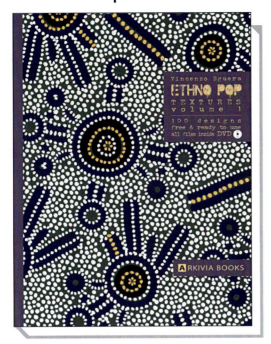

ISBN 9788888766218
HARDBACK • 112 pages
size 24cm x 30.7cm
100 TEXTURES saved
in 5 ways 500 files in all.

1 Free CD included
for WINDOWS and MAC
Vector and Bitmap Files
Ready for Production.
The use is Free

In an increasingly globalized world, creativity is becoming more and more a common heritage. Research in fashion has always drawn from cultures all over the world, reproposing for itself designs from ethnic groups which are far away in time and space.

Teen Boy Graphics vol.1

ISBN 9788888766225
HARDBACK • 96 pages
size 24cm x 30.7cm
200 GRAPHICS saved
in 4 ways-800 files in all

1 Free DVD included
for WINDOWS and MAC
Vector and Bitmap Files.

This book is the second of a series dedicated to Stylistic Studios which have produced so much creativity, applied to the market and used by countless firms. This project stems from a studio with many years of experience which has agreed to make public its fantastic work.

Ultra Pop Textures Vol.2

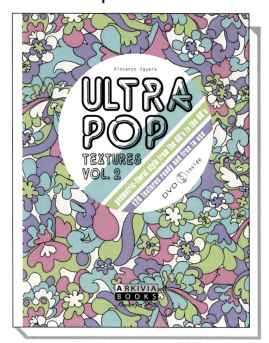

ISBN 9788888766232
HARDBACK • 144 pages
size 24cm x 30.7cm
120 TEXTURES saved
in 5 ways 600 files in all.

1 Free CD included
for WINDOWS and MAC
Vector and Bitmap Files
Ready for Production.
The use is Free

These designs describe a path which covers 3 decades from the 60's to the 80's. They highlight a very special decorative taste, at the same time refined and naif, floral and geometric in unison. Designs that communicate the rhythm of an epoch full of colours and elegance.

Animal Style Textures Vol.1

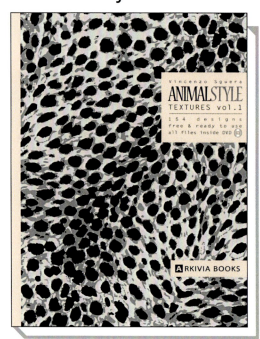

ISBN 9788888766294
HARDBACK • 160 pages
size 24cm x 30.7cm
154 TEXTURES saved
in 5 ways 770 files in all.

1 Free DVD included
for WINDOWS and MAC
Vector and Bitmap Files
Ready for Production.
The use is Free

There is a tendency that has slowly but surely imposed itself: the style inspired by animal skins. Strong, essential and recognizable it has managed to renew itself, passing from a simple proposal of natural skins to mixing these in a fresh and new way.

Logopop Volume1

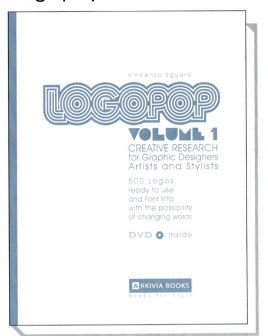

ISBN 9788888766256
HARDBACK • 160 pages
size 24cm x 30.7cm
500 LOGOS saved in 5
ways - 2500 files in all.

1 Free DVD included
for WINDOWS and MAC
Vector and Bitmap Files
Ready for Production.
The use is Free

500 Logos ready to use and font info with the possibility of changing all the words to personalize your graphics and make your own Logo!

In the panorama of books which offer thousands of Logos there has always been a lack of one with new and original designs and with the permission to use.

Ethno Pop Textures vol.2

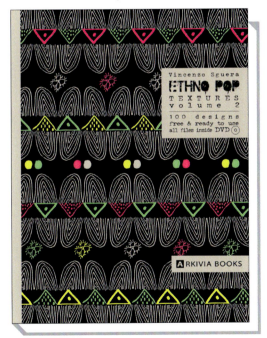

ISBN 9788888766263
HARDBACK • 112 pages
size 24cm x 30.7cm
100 TEXTURES saved
in 5 ways-500 files in all

1 Free DVD included
for WINDOWS and MAC
Vector and Bitmap Files
Ready for Production.
The use is Free

In an increasingly globalized world, creativity is becoming more and more a common heritage. Research in fashion has always drawn from

cultures all over the world, reproposing for itself designs from ethnic groups which are far away in time and space.

Natural Pop Textures Vol.2

ISBN 9788888766270
HARDBACK • 144 pages
size 24cm x 30.7cm
122 TEXTURES saved
in 5 ways 610 files in all.

1 Free DVD included
for WINDOWS and MAC
Vector and Bitmap Files
Ready for Production.
The use is Free

This second book develops more soft and elegant designs inspired by modern North-European Design also called Scandinavian Style.

New ideas in delicate colours and graphic synthesis, clean and essential, suitable for home decoration, interior design and fashion clothing textiles.

Kinetic Art Textures vol.1

ISBN 9788888766287
HARDBACK • 144 pages
size 24cm x 30.7cm
120 TEXTURES saved
in 5 ways-600 files in all

1 Free DVD included
for WINDOWS and MAC
Vector and Bitmap Files
Ready for Production.
The use is Free

Beyond the image and the meaning in every work, there are rhythm and structure to catch the aesthetics abstracted from the meaning.

The geometries have their own values apart from what they represent and they do so in a continuous and rhythmic way. This style is "KINETIC ART".